DISTURBING MUSES

Books by Mike Allen

DEFACING THE MOON
PETTING THE TIME SHARK
STRANGE WISDOMS OF THE DEAD *(forthcoming)*

As editor:

NEW DOMINIONS:
FANTASY STORIES BY VIRGINIA WRITERS

THE ALCHEMY OF STARS:
RHYSLING AWARD WINNERS SHOWCASE
(with Roger Dutcher)

DISTURBING MUSES

MIKE ALLEN

PRIME BOOKS

Disturbing Muses

Prime Books
www.prime-books.com

Acknowledgements

"Saturn Devours His Children"
first appeared in *Star*Line* 24.2, March/April 2001

"Escher's Bed"
first appeared in *Star*Line* 27.2, March/April 2004

"Miró's Mirror"
first appeared in *The Pedestal Magazine* #24, Nov. 2004

"Chagall's Lamp"
first appeared in *Strange Horizons*, March 7, 2005

"Picasso's Rapture"
first appeared in *Strange Horizons*, June 6, 2005

CONTENTS

Introduction
by Theodora Goss

The Blue Guitar

At the risk of provoking an argument, I propose: a poet never writes about a painting. "The Man With the Blue Guitar," for instance, by that strange man Wallace Stevens, is no more about Picasso's *The Old Guitarist* than it is about — petunias. It is, in a sense, more about petunias — about "things as they are," the reality that we see with our daily eyes, and the poet's relationship to that reality, those petunias. Stevens tells us that

> . . . Things as they are
> Are changed upon the blue guitar.

That is, green petunias. The blue guitar is (possibly, probably) a figure for poetry, and this, the book you are holding in your hands, is a collection of green petunias.

So. A poet writes not about the painting that his poem is ostensibly about, but about his own imaginative relationship with that painting. That strange man, Mike Allen, finds in Henri de Toulouse-Lautrec's "Streetwalker" an emissary of the Hellenic gods, wearing her "cap of Helios," as well as the ancient mask of comedy. She is Apollonian and Dionysian, both sun goddess and satyr. But her helmet is also a "teardrop," a solid, shining sadness that never falters, never falls. She is marked, after all, by the "wear and tear" of the Montmartre brothels, as well as the eternal stillness, the eternal life, into which the artist freezes his subject: both time and timelessness. A laughing, impish, grotesque and yet meaningful sorrow: that is what the poet finds, I think, in both the woman wearing her Casque d'Or and in Toulouse-Lautrec himself, in his art and his death. The poem is about the poet's perception, about what he finds in the painting and in the life. It is about his understanding. This is what he brings back to us, like an Athenian coin or the shard of a russet amphora drawn up by a fisherman from the green depths.

The Golden Helmet

Poets are born liars. And yet, I believe Mike Allen when he tells me,

> Late that afternoon,
> he is for the third time amazed
> when she kneels, silent, between his malformed legs
> to ply her trade,
> to steal a part of him away.

The golden teardrop of her hair remains solid, intact, not a strand of it disheveled or disarranged. As I believe that M.C. Escher suffered from insomnia, although the Afterword tells me (never trust a poet) that he did not. He must have, with those visions in his head, of birds becoming fish, of "the endless stair that spirals up to meet its own beginning." And so he became Procrustes, dedicated to technique, to the torture of form, with which he achieved a cold and precise perfection.

I have said, I think, that these poems are interpretations of what the poet sees on the canvas. I add that they are imaginary biographies, as true as anything that actually happened: they are biographies written the other way around, from the evidence of the art. Pablo Picasso's relationship with women, for instance, as when

> he left her a twisted, flattened shell,
> curled like wet canvas on his padded chair,
> mouth soundlessly screaming
> from the same side of her face
> that both eyes now started from.

Isn't that, don't you think it is, the way it (actually, metaphorically, what's the difference) happened? (And how unexpected: to find that Toulouse-Lautrec makes love, visually, to his muses, while Picasso, whom we thought the Don Juan of the canvas, instead destroys them.) Let us, at any rate, give Mike Allen permission to assert that it is. Because this is what a poet does, imagine the world for us. What would we do without him? Somewhere, behind the poems, behind their latticework of words, I hear him whispering,

> *And things are as I think they are*
> *And say they are on the blue guitar.*

The Disturbing Muses

Surely Escher's muse is Insomnia itself, with whom he engages in intimate intercourse, as much as Toulouse-Lautrec with his Montmartre whores. Imagine the "brutal struggle," the sheets in the morning tumbled and stained with sweat. No wonder his wife was jealous. His muse appears here in the guise of Ariadne, whose thread draws him downward to Hades, where art comes from.

For Georgia O'Keeffe it is Landscape, which she chooses over New York and Alfred Stieglitz. And this again is an interpretation, by that strange man Mike Allen: that an artist's primary relationship is with his or her art, even (or especially) when the subject of that art is another person. The artist loves his or her subject primarily as — a subject. O'Keeffe's bones, then, literalize the artist's love for what is dead, and consequently deathless. The poet tells us that Picasso's muse is Death itself. And Jackson Pollock's is surely — Chaos? How different from Escher's controlled internal landscapes:

> He gave up completely and so achieved
> complete control.

Mixing paint with the broken glass of his own accidental, alcoholic death. What the artist is in love with, finally, is always art.

You will see, of course, that Mike Allen's muses are the paintings themselves, and the artists who created them. Which makes me want to write an imaginary biography. I imagine the poet staring at the walls of a gallery, tormented by Giorgio de Chirico's *The Disturbing Muses* (those mannequins with faces like bowling pins); by Yves Tanguy's *Death Watching the Family*; by anything, anything at all, that Francisco Goya painted. It is the beginning, and perhaps the best and strangest flowering (thinking, here, of O'Keeffe's flowers, so familiar as to be unrecognizable) of modernity that so disturbs him. (Even Goya was a modern, before his time.) It is the beginning of our own age, our own mode of perception. Paul Klee, Picasso, Pollock, tell us of our own fragmentation, our own frantic motion. Marc Chagall shows us the frightening alienation (the sudden, impossible ardor) of modern love. They speak to us of our politics, as the poet speaks to us of theirs. I like to think of Mike Allen, sitting in the midst of his muses, holding his head in his hands, despairing and inspired. Don't you think that's how it happened?

The Black Hills

> She saw:
> a head of blunt teeth, empty sockets, withered hide,
> jagged-bone grin dwarfing the Black Hills' wrinkled face;
> its multitude of antlers curled
> into the space above sky,
> great branches of bone
> which could support moons as trees hold fruit.

Do you see it also? Because the book you are holding in your hands takes part in an ancient argument that began with Horace's *Ars Poetica* and his "ut pictura poesis," which means (although not literally) that poetry is similar to painting. The similarity of the "sister arts" was accepted (and seemed established) by the time Goya was born, and was challenged during his lifetime: the visual and the verbal, went the argument, were essentially different. A painting remained still, and was perceived all at once; a poem had to be read, and was perceived through time. Movement, that is, was fundamental to the poem. The arts were distant cousins, not sisters at all. And then the modernists threw all into confusion, with their Imagism, their Surrealist paintings that imply (but never tell) stories.

Notice how he tangles the argument, our poet. In a farmhouse (perhaps the one painted in *The Farm*), Joan Miró discovers a mirror, in which he sees himself and the "disembodied eyes" that watch him through a window. This is a static image (in which the painter is "transfixed" outside time), yet it is also a temporal process of understanding: he stares for "hours, days" until the world opens for him and he perceives the life in even "forks or shoes." Seeing is a process, like reading a poem. But the poem itself is filled with images: Miró in the mirror, "flat face, narrow shoulders, short timid legs," and the eyes that watch him, "in and out of frame like microbes under the lens." It is as visually complicated as *The Farm*, a series of "writhing, fluxing" lines like Miró's painting. Impossible to understand it without *seeing*. Here, let me show you a painting in motion:

> Blood-red fauns and sea-blue nymphs
> danced around his naked body and hers
> at their wedding feast.

Like the modernists, his muses, Mike Allen throws the simplicity, the elegance of "ut pictura poesis" into confusion.

The Green Petunias

But ignore me, with my interpretations and arguments. You, reader: listen to the poet play on his blue guitar, among the green petunias.

Chagall's Lamp

She shone from inside,
her skin like sunlit clouds,
her eyelashes pins of light.
He followed her, his beacon,
to escape the grey lands,
to emerge in the world each morning.

Simple man who wore
the ghosts of his beloved Vitebsk
like a comforting shawl;
because he knew they weren't ghosts at all.
Reduced to ruins by Nazi hands,
but he found it again
the first time he followed her
beyond the grey lands.

She first revealed herself to him
long years before
he left the black and white of Russia
for the kaleidoscope of Paris:
in days when his world held nothing more

than carts and cows and long school hours,
and dreams of magic-colored laughter.

At first he thought her nothing more
than his beautiful Bella
perceived in spirit by his yearning soul:
lounging nude atop
the roses on the mantle;
staring up at him from puddles,
a distaff reflection;
beheld in nighttime visions,
borne away on horses
by shadowy barbarians,
or towering anxiously over
infinities of forest where fey children played.

But he knew her to be something more
when every sighting became the same:
a shining figure cut from a summer sky,
kneeling alone, head bowed,
solemn as his mother praying at the synagogue,
a steady lamp in a vast plain of shifting grey.

She stayed with him in Moscow and Berlin,
and the creative tempest of the Paris streets.
He watched her each night, but
kept his distance, more awed than afraid.
She stayed with him, when the Stalin plague,
then the Blitzkrieg,
walled his childhood home away.

When he and Bella fled to America,
when the message came, surreal psychic telegram,
that Nazis hollowed out his beloved town;
that's when he overcame his awe,
when he spoke to her, when she stood,
beckoned him to follow
through the grey lands, past
the smiling red-eyed soldiers, past
the white crucifix leaning above the ruins.

Past all that, and there they were,
breathing in strange new space:
green-faced violin players guarding
vertical streets; carts full of children flying
above rooftops, pulled by manic nags
whose foals romped among stars;
men and women unclothed, unbound
by flesh or gravity, finding untried ways
to interlock; quiet Jews robed in earth
and light, still insisting on prayer;
winged jugglers with hummingbird heads
and wide sympathetic eyes;
all things freed of black and white
to be seen as they always truly were.
His own eyes brimming, he raised
his hands — now seven-fingered —
blew kisses to her glowing form in gratitude.

He built monuments to her in glass,
the light he knew as hers filtered

through the tints of the true universe
which he saw at first hand each night
beyond the grey lands.

The final time he followed her,
as age, infirmity, uncertainty
slipped from him like a snake's skin,
he flowed across the space between them,
touched her at last, pressed flowers
into her warm, beaming hands.

Blood-red fauns and sea-blue nymphs
danced around his naked body and hers
at their wedding feast.

The Disturbing Muses

Nodding by night around my bed,
Mouthless, eyeless, with stitched bald head.
— Sylvia Plath

A. canto d'amore

Where did he find them, stone-gowned goddesses
who half a life later would bear
silent witness as their despairing disciple
swallowed poisoned air?

In the City of the Faceless he left them,
burned the maps that charted his return,
even burned those engraved on his skin.
He peeled their lacquer from his hand
that held the brush, nailed the bleeding glove
to a wall, beneath some blind and nameless
emperor's reproachful stare.

What she could not stop herself
from embracing,
he fled.
Behind him they tracked without eyes.

One howled
from the mouth that opened between her breasts
a word
shaped in the echo chamber of her heart
with no beginning or end.

B. *malinconia della partenza*

Amnesia through repetition:
that dour drooping face presided sadly
over copy after copy;
three dummy-headed dolls, their sorcery
badly diluted through decades
of insincere self-forgery.
His detractors said he whored his past for money.
He gladly let them believe it so.
Perhaps even he believed this so;
self-mocking at the end, passing off
bleak green skies as funny,
teasing artifice, a wry prank of the soul.

But six decades before
staring up at that sick twilight
he didn't find it funny at all.
Could he recall when it became
late afternoon forever,
when the long shadows froze?
Yes: the sick pain in his belly
still unsubsided, staring at the sculpture
of Dante in the Piazza Santa Croce

when the day itself coalesced
into marble and darkness.

Hours or days, he wandered:
the light never changed.
moving enigmas, sails or trains
drifted soundless behind walls,
their cargoes hidden; he could not find
the other side, no more than he
could find a living soul.
                              Stumbling
among stark arcades, pale colonnades,
barren plazas, his survival
rested solely on an unseen denizen
who left food in incongruous places:
cluster of bananas beneath the aqueduct;
artichoke heads like war trophies
under the cannon barrel; pastries
found in places that defied the eye.

He thought, at one point, he had come
upon his savior: placed a hand on
the man's shoulder, turned him and
confronted blank mannequin face
with a single eye sketched
where brow should be.

Returned to bed, screaming,
believing he had seen the future.
The muses had made themselves known,

though he did not know it yet.
Still points of power,
triple nexus from which all stillness grew,
they awaited his arrival.

C. archeologo

Smokestacks stood watch on the horizon,
never breathing,
never close enough to touch.
Perspective was illusory
in this metaphysical space.
The profile of a face
seen outside the window
resolved itself as silhouette
of distant, impossible castle.

Still the food appeared.
Perhaps Ariadne herself —
her bare-breasted, resigned effigy
had so haunted him in Greece —
trying to lead him out of this time-twisted maze?
But every new exploration
brought him nearer to the heart, not away,
before the great red hand of the hour
swept him back.

Space made non sequitur:
Streets become walls,
tables become floors,

towers loom larger at distance
than up close. Here, entire ghettos
populated by crude mannequins;
there, mannequins as mountains,
bodies cobbled
from columned ruins.

Yet another empty piazza
beneath sinister green sky —
but what made these three blind muses
so magnify his unease?
Ruthless and primal,
stripped of all visage by the modern age.
One stood forever in shadow.
Did another shadow, smaller, dart behind?

No mouths with which to speak
but the silence itself chiseled words.

Bring us to her, it said.
Bring her to us.

A vision inside another's brain,
connected across the infinite,
transformed his own head.

D. *il sogno trasformato*

She found his painting somewhere humble,
a print in a book, stark black and white; and the same night

cowered beneath covers as three massive stone matriarchs
nodded above her knowingly. She dreamed
how their marble gowns enfolded her,
mothers' overpowering embraces.

He knew

She dreamed her own face stitched shut,
skin tanned to leather thickness, implacable ovals
for mouth and eyes, rimmed with spiraling thread;
her slender form stiff as a tailor's dummy,
her blond tresses a wig anyone could remove and wear.

What hue

She dreamed herself again risen from ashes,
another failed attempt to do what she did best;
her red-haired vengeance, like Sisyphus' stone,
always rolling back on her. Flesh, bone,
but still nothing there.

He had painted

They kept eyeless vigil around her as she prepared;
their beautiful silence grew layered, an aching harmony
that approached the perfect stillness of immutable night.
They nodded approval as she stepped into their shadows,
turned the knob and opened the altar's door.

Her life, and despaired.
Now was the future, the future from which he fled,
> *the future he fled into.*

E. enigma dell'Oracolo

He painted, and copied, and copied,
and forgot the girl of his dreams.
Married a Russian immigrant after the wars,
her slender form still as a mannequin
as she posed for his brush,
her blond tresses ghostly on the canvas.

coda: mistero di una strada

At strange street's foot
a little girl in silhouette
runs with a hoop toward
a waiting shadow
which extends its stunted limb;
blacker and heavier than she,
it grows, as she ascends,
to meet her.

Escher's Bed

Procrustes cursed him from the underworld.
No sleep ever came without brutal struggle —
his mattress seemed to tilt the wrong way,
no matter which end he laid his head upon.

Poor sleepless boy, doomed to fail school,
sent by his vexed parents to live seaside
for his health (to no avail) but the dreams,
the longing for order, for symmetry,

spilled through his hands to crystallize
in press and ink. To Jetta (poor, tolerant wife)
he blamed those ever restless nights
on Rome, on his brother's body broken

on the mountainside, on the Nazi bootprint
found marring a sketch by his murdered
Jewish mentor — while the interlocking beasts
crawling across his prints mirrored the peace

Procrustes' hex denied him. Only when he
found the impossible object, the endless stair

that spirals up to meet its own beginning,
did he understand his torment, know

that on meeting the thief in Hades,
he must stretch and shorten in one stroke
to finally fit in his own bed, beside which
his family gathered to watch him descend,

holding Ariadne's thread as it spiraled
beyond the page, into the infinite.

The Golden Helmet (*Casque d'Or*)

1. The Streetwalker

Addled in midmorning by
the fermented demons that always keep him company,
Henri staggers in his shuffling way
into *le pays des fées*
or so he thinks for a sun-blinded moment.

But, no, he's merely traipsed into
his neighbor's opulent garden, confronting
damask roses and prized white tulips
and this sinuous creature draped across
Monsieur Forest's fat lap.
A casual visitor, street wanderer
seeking new business, she is
mere flesh,
though flesh grown strange; intriguing flower
astounding his jaded eye.

Her blond locks twine up into a teardrop
that gleams with solid sheen, a golden helmet
not far removed from the priceless cap of Helios.

But no sun creature is she; it's an imp's hat
that grows from her head.
Had Bosch painted fairies, he might
have dreamed you up, thinks Henri.
An ill-used refugee from the mound, yes,
yet fey nonetheless. Wear and tear
of the kind only Montemartre brothels can induce
seam her face, her neck, but her wicked smile
smooths all into a mask of antique, even ancient mischief.

On sight of Henri she springs,
astonishes him a second time, as she takes his hand,
the one that holds the brush,
stoops to meet his eyes,
kneels to regard his palm.

A flitting fingertip traces the lines:
the contact of her skin on his
like strokes of alizarin crimson through cool green.
You are the last of your kind, she says.
A thousand years of power and darkness run in your blood.
Bad things wished to break your spirit,
but only your body could they touch, and now
you become the unrepentant fool,
the jester beloved by all the kingdom, the bonfire
that lights this mad pageant of flesh.

Dans quel vin noierons-nous ce vieil ennemi?
Dis-le, belle sorcière! says Henri,
slurring his Baudelaire.

Fey one, you have captured me. Now let me
in turn trap you forever.
                    And he painted her
in her Chinese peasant's blouse and golden helmet
as easily as a mere mortal drums his fingers
or scratches an itch.

Late that afternoon,
he is for a third time amazed
when she kneels, silent, between his malformed legs
to ply her trade,
to steal a part of him away.

2. The Circus

Such a mood etched upon him;
when he waddles into
the cafés, the dance halls,
the peepshows, the whorehouses,
when the patrons spy his stunted form,
tiny bespectacled bearded gnome,
stumps of legs supporting a grown man's torso,
and begin to laugh,
he laughs with them,
their laughter an offering he accepts,
a tribute of recognition.

He has become Montemartre's carnal spirit,
joyfully deformed,
generously corrupt,

gleefully debauched,
celebrating the body in all its pouched, plump, pocked
    imperfections,
its ringmaster and its historian,
recording the human whirlwind:
gaudy hats and billowing blouses,
the green haze of absinthe,
sagging rumps and shocks of red pubic hair,
monsieurs emerging from beneath sheets
to kiss their rented lovers,
the stark black of slumming aristocrats,
slipping away from the life he left behind for good
to test with cowardly fingers
the seething waters that were now his home.

Jester and lord in one, he sketched at the tables,
his head often cradled in the bosom
of a slender lady-in-waiting draped in fine white,
merely his due
through the short years of his reign.
Montemartre opened to him its deepest intimacies.
None turned him away.

3. The Clown

In a year, he will draw a pistol
and put bullets through the tiger-sized spiders
that will crawl out of his delirium
onto his bedroom walls.
And five after that, the success of his last

long-term undertaking: self-inflicted
death by drink.
But for now he is the darling of the press.
His wicked posters are the talk of the truly chic.

Holding court one hazy evening
among his subjects in the Rue des Moulins
he sees a glint of gold beyond the top hats,
blond hair twined into a teardrop.

His imp crowned with the sun's golden helm
fastening her bright yellow bodice,
her supple shoulderblades exposed, and more,
a tantalizing hint
closed off and concealed.
She is somehow younger, smoother,
wrapped in baggy black,
torso draped in puffy yellow cascade
that parts for a ravine of cleavage.
She is no longer a peasant but a clown, and yet
Henri can't mistake that strange flower
that so enthralled him.

She finds a bench, slumps,
legs spread wide, regards the throng with glazed eyes.
She won't remain alone long.

He wonders as he trundles her way
whether the light in her has died,
whether the poxes and opiates that collect dues at the circus door

have taken this one's toll, but no,
her gaze finds him, and there:
that infernal grin of recognition
he returns, but falters, her bared teeth
transmuted
her teeth bared, like the dead
whose lips have withered away
as she points his way
and laughs
and laughs
great mocking howls
black tears streaming down
her greased white face
beneath eyes that never blink,
and he feels again
the agony of thighbones breaking,
feels his realm flip beneath him,
Rumpelstiltskin freak whose true name lies exposed,
still the Fool, but King no more.

As she completes her theft
he swoons, stumbles to kneel
between her obscene feet, and even
though she has vanished, her laughter spreads,
surrounding him now,
gathering new voices.
Her eyes still burn,
alizarin fire
in the deep green of his drowning.

Klee's Garden

The objective world surrounding us
is not the only one possible;
there are others, latent.

Only the most beloved
of his Bauhaus pupils ever
were allowed to frolic there;
and perhaps the models who caught his eye:
Emma, Thérèse, Kathi, Mari, more —
Surely Lily knew; he denounced
painting from life years before,
though maybe his requests
were nothing so simple as amorous affairs.
(And how often did he take *her* there?
Afterward, could she speak of it?
Could she even remember?)

What strange blooms assaulted his senses
at the edge of the Sahara;
an unwise venture southward of Carthaginian ruins,
wrapped by heat that strove to turn
his flesh to paper; the miracle wind

that parted sands like so much troublesome sea;
stone temple bones protecting impossible flora,
square petals of light that, rubbed against his
vision, transmuted before his very eyes —
He dashed back from Tunisia
weeks too early, mind on fire —
The friend he left behind might also
have seen the miracle, but a French mortar shell
bought August Macke's silence.

Color has taken possession of me;
No longer must I chase after it.
I know it has hold of me forever.

The seeds, pure motes of holy hue,
sewn in the dour woods south of Weimar,
secluded even from the seclusion of his school.
At the garden grew, he meditated alone —
The Buddha of Bauhaus — coming back
with cryptic theories of design, encrypted in a grimoire
only true initiates had a hope of grasping;

perhaps that need to communicate drove him to share.
Tiny man with Rasputin's stare, mere hint
of the unearthly glow he absorbed in Africa;
As he led them on scant path through brush,
were his eager protégés ever unnerved —
their unease growing as colors amplified;

around the next turn, ancient trees reduced
to sprightly line and flimsy planes of pigment,
rippling, overlapping, mixed into new shades
by slightest puffs of air; even odder luminous growths
defining themselves against inexplicable shadows;
then the landscaping he himself applied:
cacti incongruous as tubular totems, flower pots
out of airborne boats, rows
of sawblade sun blooms; and then,
clearer moment by moment, movement:
the residents, creatures sideways from human —
Residue, perhaps, of the lucky few
he chose to let in: women with faces like blowing leaves,
men with numbers for eyes, clothed
like stop-motion phantoms;

(Beneath it all, deep underneath,
did his guests perceive the not-quite angel
with the pig-snout and pit-black orbits,
or the round-faced German whose eyes
and nose and mouth spelled "death";
or the desert itself, watching for
its chance to reclaim, to dry his flesh
from inside out, mummified in diseased agony?
He noted them from time to time
and merely instructed his wide-eyed companions
to ignore the degenerates.)

Who could then resist, when he
produced his violin and sent the notes flying

like a calculated sandstorm?
Majestic gold or courtesan blue,
flowers leapt fishlike into the air —
blocks of rainbow adobe
became spontaneous houses, temples, mosques;
bipeds covered in square scales
stood up to sing, as whimsical creatures
danced in their translucent bellies,
swallowed whole and joyous.
Among them all, he pranced,
most benevolent of all devils,
legs blurred as he scrambled up ladders,
slid down stalks, his fiddle bow
drawing mad black lines on the very
cloth of time, and he called out names
that hung rapturously beside him,
sound become tangible calligraphy.

Who could help but laugh
and clap hands in delight?
Who could help but lose themselves,
leave a piece behind?

*I cannot be understood
in purely earthly terms.*

Miró's Mirror

He discovered it, antique and strange,
in the cellar of that moss-veined farmhouse;
propped it in the corner of his secret studio,

where he stood, transfixed as Narcissus,
regarding the average, his father's forceful etching:
flat face, narrow shoulders, short timid legs,

every bit the accountant his father sculpted,
streaked by desperate stains of paint; he made
the vow, again, again, to unbind himself

from the ordinary; and through the other side,
things heard, converged from Catalan countryside,
things once seen only in dreams of peasants.

Behind him animals of line and riot
frolicked in midair; disembodied eyes opened
in blue beyond his window — never there

when he turned, but always in the glass,
too flat for any eyes but his to see, cavorting
in and out of frame like microbes under the lens.

He stared for hours, days; let them infect his retinas
till he saw, as they, how opacity of walls or skin
were mere parlor tricks, how his face, his house,

the farm outside, the world itself stood open
as the sky; how life's residual glow, bright corona,
clings to possessions simple as forks or shoes.

On the fourth night he went to sleep starving
and they invaded his dreams. Next morning,
the mirror gone, but from then on, they followed

in window reflections, in puddles, in corners
of a watering eye, shape shifting entourage,
endless carnival in orbit around his grasping soul.

He welcomed them, longed his life to join
their number, trade his skin for writhing, fluxing line,
unwinding hues which can no more be contained

than pagan dances of the frenzied spirit.

O'Keeffe's Bones

To me they are strangely more living
than the animals walking around . . .
They cut sharply to the center of something
keenly alive — vast, empty, untouchable —
that knows no kindness with its beauty.

No god could survive in the desert.
But dead gods
still can desire. Speak. Scheme.

They watched this small woman,
her black hair pulled back taut,
her easels and determined paints,
her square face and gaze
deep as the endless horizon.

They watched this small fierce woman
who did not know them, yet still drawn
away from the claustrophobic loveliness of Lake George,
from the claustrophobic darkness of New York,
from Alfred's claustrophobic love.

They spoke to her in subtleties.
In black rocks, beveled cliffs, bleached ivory.
They schemed in sand red as raw flesh.
Undaunted by the stark Catholic crosses
that captured her eye,
they chose their moment.

She saw:
a head of blunt teeth, empty sockets, withered hide,
jagged-bone grin dwarfing the Black Hills' wrinkled face;
its multitude of antlers curled
into the space above sky,
great branches of bone
which could support moons as trees hold fruit.
Sky gathered thunderheads in a mantle,
soaked the emptiness
beneath its rolling cloak,
spoke of beauty in fragments,
of love scoured clean of the mortal,
of the perfection of the faraway,
majestic and sad as skeletal landscapes,
from which she never fully returned.

From her Ghost Ranch
she worshiped
and in the end worshiped alone,
her faith enough to flood a desert
with umber, to send black rivers
to fill cracks in stone,

to saturate sands
with the cooling blue of night;
to give driest rock
the vitality of arterial blood.

Picasso's Rapture

Aphrodite is exacting a tribute of me for all my race.
    — Ovid, *Heroides*

1. *une femme*

There is no abstract art.
You must always start
with something. Afterwards
you can remove all traces of reality.

By the time of their meeting, he
was indeed a Master.
Removing her reality
took no more effort
than sketching a face on air.

The Minotaur's passion sated,
he left her a twisted, flattened shell,
curled like wet canvas on his padded chair,
mouth soundlessly screaming
from the same side of her face
that both eyes now started from.

He sighed in satisfaction,
then began the erasure.
Soon, no one there.
As with many before her.
He had not learned her name,
and did not care.

2. *son visage bleu*

Casagemas' head protruded
from the sheet that wrapped his
body; eyelids swollen,
temple stained black with
gunpowder, skin blue and
waxen in the candlelight.

Pablo watched them bear away
his best friend from Barcelona,
slain by a woman's refusal
as surely as she'd tugged his
fingers on the pistol with
puppet strings. Pablo knew
then: all women are witches.
Only an equal sorcerer
can survive them.

When the scarlet fever delirium
claimed him from Madrid,
he had lain in a down-stuffed bed
in a Catalan mountain villa,

staring through a narrow window
at the verdant slopes; things seen
in that haze, shapes cavorting
in midair, opening doors
that weren't there, opening
space to show him views
from all angles at once.
Memories gnawed at the back
of his grieving brain: how to
find again that visionary state,
force it to obey his desires?

Until he found the first hints,
Casagemas' blue face swelled
behind every new encounter.

3. *l'Arlequin*

Some claim he infused those
thousands of canvasses with
hidden arcana, invocations
au culte mithraïque, tributes
to the god who slew
the celestial bull; had he heard,
Pablo would have laughed,
and rightly so, for the only alchemy
fused into his creations
was a magic he alone invented.

Against the skin of Fernande,
his first mistress, and first woman
he would claim to truly love,
the rapture of seeing outside
space returned, this time
to a clear, unfevered mind,
and he knew he could be
the new Harlequin, protégé
of trickster Hermes, author
of any wizardry his lusts demanded.

He painted himself,
handsome, sullen, clad in
diamonds of rose and black,
wearing Harlequin's peaked hat,
the nature of his magic
as yet unsculpted. He filled
the following years with a quest
for final configurations,
sharpened the vision that saw
from all sides at once, allowing
him to shape others to his whim.

And at last he shed
the Harlequin's chequered skin;
pierced and thrown away
with the toss of a horn
as he assumed the form
(distilled from the arenas
of Spain) that suited him best.

4. *Minotauromachia*

Do all women harbor an need
for annihilation? Most would deny it
but if one did yearn, he would find her,
smell her an auction hall away,
taste her scent amid hundreds
in the newly-opened gallery,
home in on her through
crowded streets; the Minotaur
weaving toward its meal.

As helpless as Europa draped
across the bull, she would come
to where he led, brook no struggle
as the Beast compressed,
flattened, conformed her
to its all-consuming vision.

*Why not the genitals
in place of the eyes,
and the eyes between the legs?*

Even those whom he allowed
names, whom he spared
the Bull's machinations:
what of them? One hanged,
two driven insane, one shooting
herself (just as Casagemas);
others that survived live on
only in the story he painted.

5. *son seul amour vrai*

How to reconcile the cocky hero
whose heart tore at the thought
of a Basque village bombed,
who painted a protest of
war's horrors, pressed postcards
of that protest into the hands
of Nazi soldiers, and yet
was never arrested; could the same
man be the Beast who tore
scores of women into surreal
contortions, and casually disposed
of the remains? Could one
divide himself so completely
into parallel planes?

Though he once imagined it so,
no avenging angel with hawk beak
and barrel chest ever descended
to stuff the Minotaur back
in his Harlequin cloak, bear
the wailing creature away.

Though he uttered the word
too many times to count,
only one woman truly earned
his adoration. As he lounged
in the Chateau Vauvenargue,
he recognized her form,

sensuous curves out of his
deepest dreams, drawing into
focus. He readied himself
for the one mistress
that remained to conquer
or at last be bested by,
knowing he loved her truly,
knowing she loved him even more.

I think of Death all the time.
She is the only woman
who never leaves me.

Pollock's Knives

He fell into the painting — Jack the Dripper
poured his self out, used broken glass
to thicken the medium, attacked the surface
from all four sides. The careening convertible

at last came to a stop, but he did not, not yet —
his blood so much flying pigment,
quicksilver droplets, suspended —
He gave up completely and so achieved
complete control.
                    He fell into the painting
that opened around him in all directions.
He fell into the universe of his dying,
god and sacrifice all in one.
                        Was his goddess
any where to be found, the moon woman
with crescent pupils, who tore apart the circle
of her own binding while he watched?

His mistress would survive the car crash.
His wife would survive the wreck of his life.
His last thoughts in this world weren't
for them at all.

* * *

He had at last found what to do
when he couldn't paint:
a proper death for an American celebrity,
cementing immortality by casting life aside.
He controlled the ebb and flow,
but things always changed
once they struck the surface.

* * *

Broiling boy, never knew
a home, a place; if

a surface seemed stable, he would
assault it, abrade it,
shatter it, shred the pieces.
Struggling mother, Stella tried
to harness his fury, focus it
on canvas. But a canvas
couldn't cry out in pain.
His life a chaos of turbulence,
something vulnerable always
bleeding at its off-center.

Fight in a Los Angeles alley,
this one involved knives.
The small Mexican boy
had black eyes, coal black,

(no whites) and two arms
too many to defend against;
vanished, left his blades broken
off in 16-year-old Paul's
screaming flanks (that name, Paul,
he would later shed) but no one else
could see the wounds he claimed were there;
or they would not admit it,
no matter how he insisted.

An art school in New York:
as far away from those black orbs as he could go.

* * *

The alcohol forever walled away
the memory of that strange encounter
but not its effects.

He tried to bleed himself.
Relieve the piercing pressure
that wormed in deeper every day.
At first he didn't know the way.

He searched Mexican murals,
with their dark-eyed martyrs,
though he didn't understand what answer
he was looking for.

When Miró's phantasms and Picasso's distortions
erupted in the museum halls,
he felt resonance, kinship, a sense
of distance closed, of surfaces gone brittle,
primed to be shattered.

The alcohol walled the ways,
but rage superceded stupor, forced him
to climb, search blind
for the way to bleed himself.

* * *

She didn't look human, couldn't have been,
creature whose face
was the moon turned away from the sun.
(Afterward, he would paint her,
though he couldn't articulate her form,
understood it wasn't wise to try.)
Sigils of constellations
coalesced at her back
into a word he could not fathom.
How deep had he crawled inside himself,
to find her here?

She was bound inside a circle of her own making,
or of his: a sense of struggle, frozen, poised,
but then something —
the essence of a knife, blurred blade
in the abstraction of her hand.

51

The circle lashed away, snapped free,
crumpling to a flowing loop of blood-black.

She stared at him and at the same time stared away
through an eye with a bright crescent pupil
and an eye limned like ink scratched on sun
before dissolving into splotches, trickling off
and gone.
                    He did not love her.
But knew in his cells what her message meant.

I will bleed all colors.
                         I will control
the ebb and flow. I will paint with knives.

                          * * *

He tried to fall through the floor of his barn,
dripping, seeping across canvas after canvas,
attacking from all sides, slicing the excess
until only the perfect window remained,
or nothing at all. The ache left
for three beautiful years, happy years without walls.

But the blades did not come free,
would not; though he poured out more than
he could ever contain, something tainted remained.
The ache returned, then the walls.
In the end he could not paint at all.

                          * * *

And at last he found what to do
when he couldn't paint.
No color was sufficient surrogate
for the hue he knew he had to use
to cremate the memory of black eyes.

As he tore apart the circle of his own binding,
did crescents open in his new sky?

His last thoughts in transition
plunged through an endless —
flooded with layer on layer
of streaking stars, seeping galaxies.
Things vast and multi-limbed
loomed beyond the edge, quasar echoes.

His last thoughts in transition
weren't human thoughts at all.
Things always changed
once they broke the surface.

Saturn Devours His Children

El sueño de la razón produce monstruos.
— Francisco Goya

I watch the black goat-man dance around the fire
before spirits twisted with fear-filled desire.
I can't hear their manic laughter, but I see —
through the walls of this house I see their screams.

Leocadia, my dearest, who would now believe
you are the same beauty for whom I once risked death,
my ageless Maja of supple thighs and soft pale breasts
for whose image the Inquisitor wished me charred

two long decades ago? Perhaps he knew the sin in you
ran deeper than bare hips and mischievous eyes.
Infernal one, Leocadia was never your name,
but your true name I will not learn, so it will do.

Observe these two old men that I have placed
beside the window, how one leans close, his lips
brush so intimately beneath the other's ear.
These phantoms, etched in dust on void,

are you and I, Leocadia . . . but it's you who tilts
your head as if to listen, and I who drains soul's nectar
from your neck. What small sacrifice I have made
for your sweetly cursed sorcery, this sight that left me deaf

but lights the universe's secret shadows bright
as solstice moons, shows me the giant whose footsteps
toppled cities of Spain, the djinn who battle in the clouds
for our souls, the monsters that flap from our heads

when we sleep. I marvel, my Leocadia, at your contentment.
Playing my mad muse feeds you more, it seems,
than the hordes of souls who have served as your wine
in the banquet of dreams. If you chose me, one night,

Leocadia, as your partner, offered me death in your arms,
let me shudder out my life against your unearthly flesh,
I would gladly come. But you will not make prey, you
say, of one you truly love. My death, you leave to another.

As I bring your fingertips to my lips, dearest one, I wonder
what alien thoughts must swim behind those timeless eyes,
as you watch old man Saturno gnaw your love away,
as Time most surely devours all his mortal children.

Tanguy's Pebble

They thought de Chirico granted him the gift, and he
allowed everyone to believe, because the truth was far
too strange. He never shared it, not even with Kay,
until too late:

parted from his ship off the Argentine coast,
stolen by the sea gods, delivered, thirsty and freezing,
into the shadow of the Patagonian forest, where a serpent
like coils of fire punctured him in greeting; overhead

the arboreal sea rolled, as he crawled in delirium
over rocky mounds like glowing coral, slipped with a gasp
into sudden grottos, into a world of air like water, of wonders:

beings of plasma and stone; ribbons of curling intellect distilled
from form or purpose; entities of gem-hued mercury flowing
against each other in couplings of love or death; up or down

cast away like masts in a storm, no horizon, unbounded chasm,
warm gold-green stretching beyond sight; he swum, spun,
center of new cosmos, observer of infinities, himself observed —

a small thing, a pebble of liquid, no larger than a lima bean
drifted near, hovered at his fingertips like an inquisitive cat.
Anemone in miniature, his fingers closed — he felt little more
than a soap-bubble burst; fingers splayed again, the pebble gone.

All warmth extinguished. The universe, a roiling blue abyss.
Great hairy worm-things squealed, bleeding clouds of octopus
     ink.
Needle pyramids stabbed the void; wires like marionette strings
grew from nowhere, angled toward him, groped for his limbs.

He fled, in no direction and all, steered by fear beyond
     understanding,
to rouse, thrashing, in sheets soaked with ocean brine sweat;
     daylight
leaned in over the strange adobe arches of Rio Gallegos. Naked,
he stood before the mirror, a sea-hardened merchant mariner,
     Bible

perched by the basin like an accusation; stood, watched
     movement
beneath his skin, a throbbing lump the size of a pebble,
     submerged
into the meat below his wrist. No pain in his flesh, but an ache
that grew, a wanderlust no longer sated by waves against a hull

or foreign ports filled with women of exotic skins. His return
to Paris failed to ease that formless urge, till he read Breton,
felt hope stir. At first his efforts were crude, amateur-Dali,
but his pebbled hand, no matter how he fought, grew more sure,

opening windows to boundless regions he began to see
as home: underwater dreamscapes, crawling crystal cities,
peopled with animalcules of molten stone. He married
     troubled Kay,
herself adrift, who sensed how his soul trawled the deeps,

but couldn't share his mercurial bond, her paintings imperfect
refractions of that subtidal realm. Yet powers there sensed
their congregation of two, warned them of what leered from
over the Alsace; he saw it in the midst of a picnic, black cloud

hovering in the east, grinning, amoebic, exploded cubist skull —
or perhaps a different warning caused his westward flight.
Ensconced in America, he forced his dreams a different way,
exchanging water and crystal for desert and meshing line,

a new space where, perhaps, he hoped to slip away when
the marionette wires latched to him at last; resigned, homesick,
he put up no fight as they dragged him away, leaving poor Kay
to pore in confusion over the quicksilver pebble left behind,

that lodged in her arid dreams like the bullet
in her broken heart.

Afterword

The seeds of these poems first cracked open in my pre-teen years, I suppose, when I developed a fascination with "Modern Art" — "modern" in this context referring to the era of Cubism and Surrealism — and spent hours poring over the plates in books about Picasso and Dali. The actual writing of these poems feels to me like a sort of circular creative melding, as the things I mooned over as a boy now mesh with my adult (if not precisely "grown-up") dreamings.

As for how they are assembled: a combination of research and imaginings, based on an idea that many of these Masters' sublime abstractions in fact depict real things; which, in their way, they do. My own subjective reactions to the paintings, and in some cases details entirely of my own invention, such as Escher's insomnia, are liberally mixed in. Sometimes a single painting sparked a piece; sometimes just a general affinity for the artist. The titles always came first, then the verses themselves.

A list of all the paintings used to inspire these poems would be far too long to include here. Here's a partial inventory: Marc Chagall's "Bride with a Fan," "The Juggler" and "Birthday"; Georgio de Chirico's "The Disturbing Muses," "Love Song" and "Mystery and Melancholy of a Street"; Henri de Toulouse-Lautrec's "The Streetwalker," "Rue des Moulins" and "Seated

Clown"; M.C. Escher's "Ascending and Descending"; Paul Klee's "Botanical Theater," "The Golden Fish" and "Death and Fire"; Joan Miró's "The Farm," "Harlequin's Carnival" and "Still Life with Old Shoe"; Georgia O'Keeffe's "From the Faraway Nearby"; Pablo Picasso's "Death of Casagemas," "Harlequin with a Glass," "Minotauromachia" and a sketch for the stage production "La 14 Juillet" in which Harlequin and Minotaur are one; Jackson Pollock's "The Moon-Woman Cuts the Circle"; Francisco Goya's "The Maja Nude," "The Colossus" and all of the Black Paintings; Yves Tanguy's "Mama, Papa is Wounded!" and "Death Watching the Family"; and within the Tanguy poem, de Chirico's "The Child's Brain."

I hope you seek out these works, and that they puzzle and fascinate you, as they have me.

— Mike Allen, July 2005

Aside from the artists whose names were pilfered to give these poems their titles, a number of folks have done duty as Muses for this book and deserve note: Sonya Taaffe, who pushed for this book to be made, and Sean Wallace, who listened to Sonya; Dora Goss, who went above and beyond to paint me with petunias; Ian Watson, my brother-sage across the Atlantic, whose input always makes me look much smarter than I actually am; Sam Dean, whose suggestion of a side trip to the Metropolitan Museum of Art led to a creative explosion; Lindsay Durango, poet buddy, who helped proof; Cathy Reniere, good friend, for her steady support, and Shirl Sazynski, for first suggesting this book should be; the editors — Bruce Boston, Roger Dutcher, David C. Kopaska-Merkel, Tim Pratt — who showcased some of these poems before their appearance here; and finally, Anita, my light, my heart, my all, who knows what it's really like to have me around, but still keeps me.

By day, **MIKE ALLEN** works as a newspaper reporter covering court cases; in his spare time, he serves as both President of the Science Fiction Poetry Association and editor of the speculative poetry journal *Mythic Delirium*. He first caught the poetry bug in earnest in 1994, while working toward his master's degree in creative writing at Hollins University; since then, he's had well over 100 poems published in places such as *Asimov's Science Fiction*, *Jabberwocky*, *Strange Horizons*, and *Weird Tales*. In 2003, he shared a Rhysling Award with Charles Saplak for their collaborative poem "Epochs in Exile: A Fantasy Trilogy." A longer collection of his poetry and fiction, *Strange Wisdoms of the Dead*, is forthcoming from Prime Books.

Mike's first stint as an editor came in 1995, when he published *New Dominions: Fantasy Stories by Virginia Writers*, with contributions by writers including Nelson Bond and R.H.W. Dillard. Most recently, he co-edited *The Alchemy of Stars: Rhysling Award Winners Showcase*, which for the first time collects the Rhysling Award-winning poems from 1978 to 2004 in one volume.

He lives in Roanoke, Va., with his wife, Anita, two comical dogs and a diabolical cat. His website is **www.descentintolight.com**.

THEODORA GOSS' short stories and poems have appeared in such publications as *Alchemy*, *Polyphony*, *Realms of Fantasy*, and *Strange Horizons*, and have been reprinted in several "Year's Best" anthologies. Her prose poem "Octavia is Lost in the Hall of Masks," first published in *Mythic Delirium*, won a Rhysling Award in 2004. This year, her story "The Wings of Meister Wilhelm" is a World Fantasy Award nominee. A chapbook of her short stories and poems, *The Rose in Twelve Petals and Other Stories*, is available from Small Beer Press, and a short story collection, *In the Forest of Forgetting*, is forthcoming from Prime Books. Visit her website at **www.theodoragoss.com**.

www.ingramcontent.com/pod-product-compliance
Lightning Source LLC
Chambersburg PA
CBHW030829060726
47590CB00004B/1457